1

2

3

Found By Him.

By

John C Burt.

4

Photographs Courtesy of :

wolfgang - hasselmann.
white - rainforest.
frankie - lopez.
dimitry - zub.
gabriel - tovar.
travel now - or - crylater.
miguel - a - amutio.
tim - foster.
Free downloads :
   unsplash.com

Foreword :

And so we begin this very book; ' Found By Him?' It is all about being found by the Lord Jesus Christ as the very Shepherd of your

22

Body, Mind and Spirit! In the Biblical Record we are over and over again and again presented with the imagery of the Lord God Almighty as the Shepherd of the Sheep; His Sheep?

23

Within the very
pages of this book
we will all take a
journey of
discovery through
some of the verses
that have to do
with this Shepherd
imagery in the
Word of God! In
the end, it's all ...

with the prayers
and the hopes
that you too will
be or become
counted among
the very sheep of
the very pastures
of the Lord Jesus
Christ, the Father
and the Holy
Spirit ?

As you would know there are already many, many sheep of the very pastures of the Lord Jesus Christ, the Father and the very Holy Spirit in the World - at - Large? Yet,

26

there needs to be more and more sheep who will come to graze upon these pastures. As one considers the numbers of sheep that we use as farm animals; one can get an idea of the numbers involved; the numbers of human beings involved is even greater?

When one is found by the Shepherd of one's spirit, mind and body, one comes

28

Home to the ONE who truly has ownership of one? The ONE TRUE LORD GOD is the ONE who is CREATOR of every human being on the planet and therefore has ownership! My ..

point, is that,
there is no other
Spiritual force, or
gods who has the
right of
ownership over
every human
being on the
planet! Rather,
the right of
ownership belongs

to the ONE TRUE LORD GOD ALMIGHTY; THE FATHER, THE SON and THE VERY HOLY SPIRIT! This is an idea that we will all discuss and consider at some length in the very course of this book?

31

Also, this very book will consider why it is so important to be 'Found By Him?' What it can and does mean in reality to be found by him; in terms..

of one's own life and it's ultimate destination and endpoint! There is much to be said for being and becoming a Sheep of the pastures of the Lord God Almighty; Life really begins truly then!

33

1.

We will now begin the citations from the Word of ..

God. Three different versions will be used; they will be the ESV, the GNT and the NIV translations?

{ ESV }

Psalm 23 :

The LORD Is My Shepherd :

A Psalm of David

" (1) The LORD is my shepherd; I shall not want.

(2) He makes me lie down in green pastures.

He leads me beside still waters.

49

(3) He restores my soul. He leads me in paths of righteousness for his name's sake. (4) Even though I walk through the valley of the shadow of death,

I will fear
no evil,
    for you are
with me;
    your rod
and your staff,
    they comfort
me.
    (5) You
prepare a table
before me

in the
presence of my
enemies;
you anoint
my head with oil;
my cup overflows.
(6) Surely
goodness and
mercy
shall follow
me

52

all the days
of my life,
and I shall
dwell in the house
of the LORD
forever. " "

I Am the Good Shepherd :

" (1) " Truly, truly, I say to you, he who does not enter the ...

56

sheepfold by the door but climbs in by another way, that man is a thief and a robber.

(2) But he who enters by the door is the shepherd of the sheep.

(3) To him the gatekeeper opens. The sheep hear his voice, and he calls his own sheep by name and leads them out.

(4) When he has brought out all his own, he ...

goes before them, and the sheep follow him, for they know his voice. (5) A stranger they will not follow, but they will flee from him, for they do not know the voice of strangers. "

(6) This figure of speech Jesus used with them, but they did not understand what he was saying to them.

(7) So Jesus again said to them, "Truly, truly,

60

I say to you, I am the door of the sheep.

(8) All who came before me are thieves and robbers, but the sheep did not listen to them.

(9) I am the door. If anyone

enters by me, he
will be saved and
will go in and out
and find pasture.
(10) The
thief comes only to
steal and kill and
destroy. I came
that they may
have life and have
it abundantly.

(11) I am the good shepherd. The good shepherd lays down his life for the sheep.

(12) He who is a hired hand and not a shepherd, who does not own the

sheep, sees the
wolf coming and
leaves the sheep
and flees, and the
wolf snatches
them and scatters
them.

(13) He
flees because he is
a hired hand and
cares nothing for ..

the sheep.

    (14) I am the good shepherd. I know my own and my own know me,

    (15) just as the Father knows me and I know the Father; and I lay down ..

my life for the sheep.

(16) And I have other sheep that are not of this fold. I must bring them also, and they will listen to my voice. So there will be ..

one flock, one shepherd.

(17) For this reason the Father loves me, because I lay down my life that I may take it up again.

(18) No one takes it from

me, but I lay it
down of my
accord. I have
authority to lay it
down, and I have
authority to take
it up again. This
charge I have
received from my
Father. " "

68

Luke 15 : 1 - 7:

The Parable of
the Lost Sheep :

" (1) Now
the tax collectors
and sinners were
all drawing near...

72

to hear him.

(2) And the Pharisees and the scribes grumbled, saying, " This man receives sinners and eats with them. "

(3) So he told them this ...

parable:

(4) " What man of you, having a hundred sheep, if he has lost one of them, does not leave the ninety - nine in the open country, and go after the

one that is lost,
until he finds it?

(5) And when
he has found it, he
lays it on his
shoulders, rejoicing.

(6) And when
he comes home, he
calls together his
friends and his
neighbors, saying to
them, ' Rejoice with

me, for I have
found my sheep
that was lost.'

(7) Just
so, I tell you,
there will be much
joy in heaven over
one sinner who
repents than over
ninety - nine
righteous persons

76

who need no
repentance." "

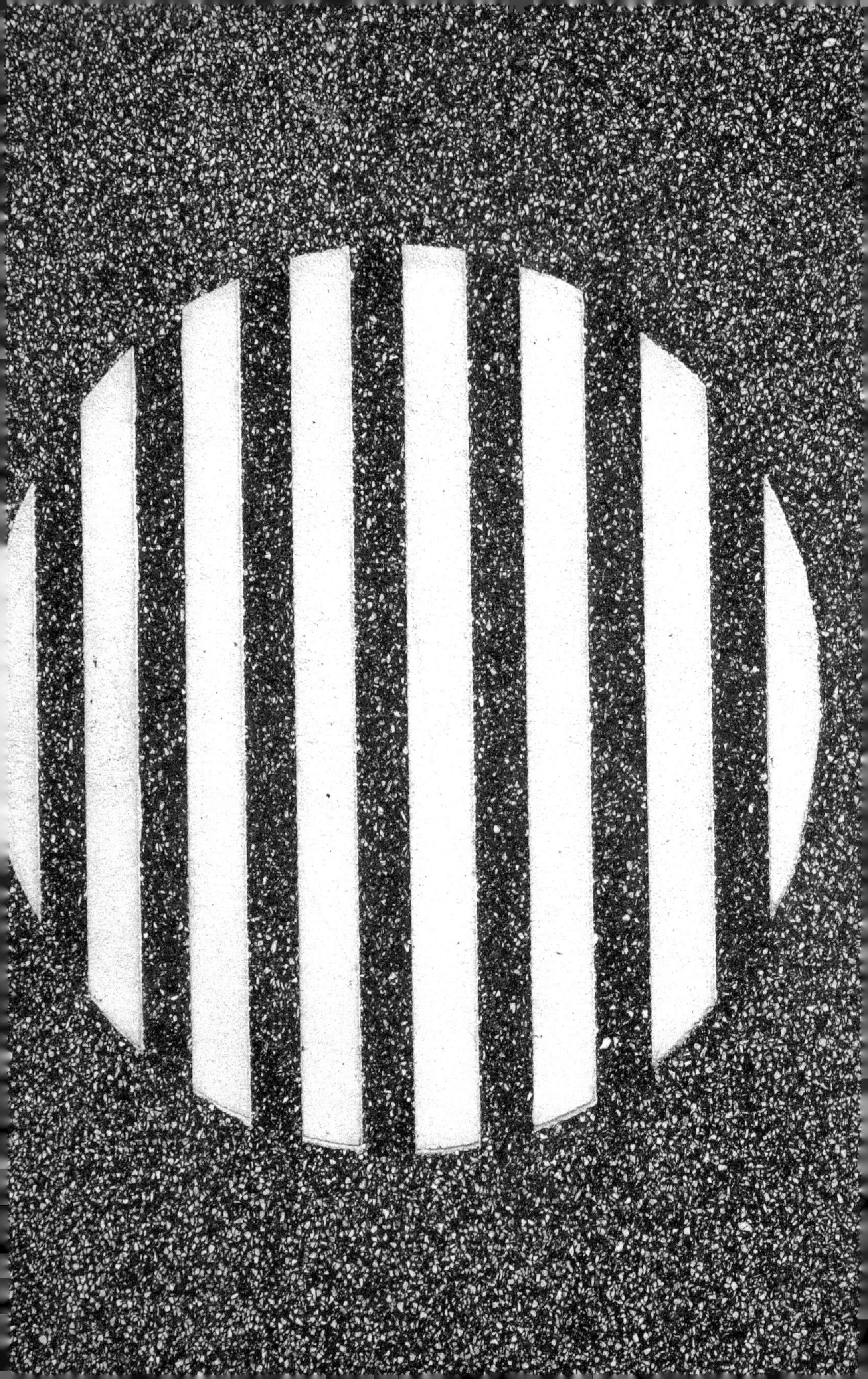

2.

{ GNT }

Psalm 23:

86

The LORD Our
Shepherd :

" (1) The
LORD is my
shepherd;
    I have
everything I need.
    (2) He
lets me rest in
fields of green ...

grass

and leads me
to quiet pools of
fresh water.

(3) He
gives me new
strength.

He guides
me in the right
paths,

as he has

promised.

(4) Even if I go through the deepest darkness, I will not be afraid, LORD, for you are with me. Your shepherd's rod ..

89

and staff protect
me.

    (5) You
prepare a banquet
for me,
      where all
my enemies can
see me;
      you welcome
me as a honored
guest

90

and fill my
cup to the brim.
(6) I
know that your
goodness and love
will be with me
all my life;
and your
house will be my
home as
long as I live. " "

91

John 10 : 1 - 18:

The Parable of
the Shepherd :

" (1) Jesus
said, " I am
telling you the
truth: the man ..

94

who does not
enter the sheep
pen by the gate,
but climbs in
some other way,
is a thief and a
robber.

(2) The
man who goes in
through the gate
is the shepherd

of the sheep.

(3) The gatekeeper opens the gate for him; the sheep hear his voice as he calls his own sheep by name, and he leads them out.

(4) When he has brought ..

96

them out, he goes ahead of them, and the sheep follow him, because they know his voice.

(5) They will not follow someone else; instead, they will run away from ..

such a person,
because they do
not know his
voice. "

(6) Jesus
told them this
parable, but they
did not understand
what he meant.

Jesus the Good
Shepherd :

(7) So
Jesus said again,
" I am telling
you the truth: I
am the gate for
the sheep.
(8) All
others who came

before me are thieves and robbers, but the sheep did not listen to them.

(9) I am the gate. Those who come in by me will be saved; they will come in and go out and ...

100

find pasture.

(10) The thief comes only in order to steal, kill, and destroy. I have come in order that you might have life - life in all its fullness.

(11) " I am

the good
shepherd, who is
willing to die for
the sheep.

(12) When
the hired man,
who is not a
shepherd and
does not own the
sheep, sees a wolf
coming, he leaves

the sheep and runs away; so the wolf snatches the sheep and scatters them.

(13) The hired man runs away because he is only a hired man and does not care about the sheep.

(14-15) I am the good shepherd. As the Father knows me and I know the Father, in the same way I know my sheep and they know me. And I am willing

to die for them.
(16) There are other sheep which belong to me that are not in this sheep pen. I must bring them, too; they will listen to my voice, and they will become one..

flock with one shepherd.

(17) " The Father loves me because I am willing to give up my life, in order that I may receive it back again.

(18) No one takes my life

away from me. I give it up of my own free will. I have the right to give it up, and I have the right to take it back. This is what my Father has commanded me to do." "

Luke 15 : 1 - 7:

The Lost Sheep:

" (1) One day when many tax collectors and other outcasts came to listen to Jesus,

110

(2) the Pharisees and the teachers of the Law started grumbling, ' This man welcomes outcasts and even eats with them!"

(3) So Jesus told them ..

111

this parable:

(4) "Suppose one of you has a hundred sheep and loses one of them - what do you do? You leave the other ninety - nine sheep in the pasture and go looking for the ..

one that got lost until you find it.

(5) When you find it, you are so happy that you put it on your shoulders

(6) and carry it back home. Then you call your friends

and neighbors
together and say
to them,' I am so
happy I found my
lost sheep. Let us
celebrate! '

(7) In the
same way, I tell
you, there will be
more joy in heaven
over one sinner ...

114

who repents than over ninety - nine respectable people who do not need to repent. " "

3.

{ NIV }

Psalm 23 :

A psalm of David:

" (1) The LORD is my shepherd, I lack nothing.

(2) He makes me lie down in green pastures,

he leads

me beside quiet
waters,
        (3) he
refreshes my
soul.
        He guides
me along the
right paths
        for his
name's sake.
        (4) Even

though I walk
through the
darkest valley, I
will fear no evil.
     for you are
with me;
     your rod
and your staff
they comfort me.
     (5) You
prepare a table ..

129

before me
in the presence
of my enemies.
You anoint
my head with oil;
my cup
overflows.

(6) Surely
your goodness and
love will follow me
all the days of my

130

life,
   and I will
dwell in the
house of the
LORD forever." "

John 10 : 1 - 18 :

The Good Shepherd and His Sheep :

" (1) " Very truly I tell you Pharisees, anyone

who does not
enter the sheep
pen by the gate,
but climbs in by
some other way, is
a thief and a
robber.

(2) The
one who enters by
the gate is the
shepherd of the ..

sheep.

(3) The gatekeeper opens the gate for him, and the sheep listen to his voice. He calls his own sheep by name and leads them out.

(4) When

he has brought
out all his own,
he goes on ahead
of them, and his
sheep follow him
because they
know his voice.
      (5) But
they will never
follow a stranger;
in fact, they will

run away from him because they do not recognize a stranger's voice."

(6) Jesus used this figure of speech, but the Pharisees did not understand what he was telling them.

(7)Therefore Jesus said again, " Very truly I tell you, I am the gate for the sheep.

(8) All who have come before me are thieves and robbers, but the sheep have not listened to them.

(9) I am the gate; whoever enters through me will be saved. They will come in and go out, and find pasture.

(10) The thief comes only to steal and kill and destroy; I ...

140

have come that
they may have
life, and have it
to the full.

(11) "I
am the good
shepherd. The
good shepherd
lays down his life
for the sheep.

(12) The hired hand is not the shepherd and does not own the sheep. So when he sees the wolf coming, he abandons the sheep and runs away. Then the wolf attacks the

flock and scatters
it.

(13) The
man runs away
because he is a
hired hand and
cares nothing for
the sheep.

(14) " I
am the good
shepherd; I know

my sheep and my
sheep know me -
(15) just
as the Father
knows me and I
know the Father -
and I lay down
my life for the
sheep.
(16) I
have other sheep

that are not of this sheep pen. I must bring them also. They too will listen to my voice, and there shall be one flock and one shepherd.

(17) The reason my Father

loves me is that I lay down my life - only to take it up again.

(18) No one takes it from me, but I lay it down of my own accord. I have authority to lay it down and authority

146

to take it up
again. This
command I
received from my
Father." "

Luke 15 : 1 - 7 :

The Parable of
the Lost Sheep :

" (1) Now
the tax collectors
and sinners were
all gathering
around to hear ...

150

Jesus.

(2) But the Pharisees and the teachers of the law muttered, " This man welcomes sinners and eats with them. "

(3) Then Jesus told them ..

this parable:

(4) "Suppose one of you has a hundred sheep and loses one of them. Doesn't he leave the ninety - nine in the open country and go after the lost sheep until he ...

finds it?

(5) And when he finds it, he joyfully puts it on his shoulders

(6) and goes home. Then he calls his friends and neighbors ....

together and says,
' Rejoice with me;
I have found my
lost sheep.'
(7) I tell
you that in the
same way there
will be be more
rejoicing in heaven
over one sinner
who repents than

over ninety - nine
righteous persons
who do not need
to repent. " "

4.

Psalm 23 and being 'Found By Him?'

172

In so many ways I love the 23rd Psalm; it has much to say to us all. This is also true of the theme of being; ' Found By Him'; and it's ..... implications for us all? Essentially, one has to already be a

sheep of the
' Shepherd of the
Soul's'; for the 23rd
Psalm and it's
many outlines and
benefits from the
Shepherd and
being one of His
sheep to become
true and real.
          The bottom -

line of the 23rd Psalm, is that, it is the One who is the ' Shepherd of the Soul's of His Sheep' ; who provides, cares for and looks out for the sheep who know Him. The shepherd makes sure that the sheep under His care, His sheep are provided for and receive the care they need? He provides them with sustenance and great pastures where they can feed and feel secure and safe in.

176

The Lord God Almighty; the Father, the Son of God and the very Holy Spirit are the 'Shepherds of the Soul's of their Sheep?' There is a real protection and safety in being one of their sheep; a ..

sheep that belongs to their sheepfold and is a part of their greater flock of sheep. This is true whatever comes or goes in one's life and as one seeks to live out one's life before the gaze of the Lord

God Almighty. It is true and a truism no matter whether your life and times are full of darkness, storms or sunshine and ease? The reality, is that, the 'Shepherd of the Soul's' cares for His sheep whatever the very circumstances may be in one's life and times. There is a promise that the 'Shepherd of the Soul's' will be there in the darkness and the rough times that are hard to handle for the sheep.

To be a sheep of the 'Shepherd of the Soul's' is also to be protected and kept safe from the enemies of one as well. Sheep and the flock's of sheep can be and are attacked by many

181

things. It is right in the midst of these enemies of the sheep and one's soul that the very 'Shepherd of the Soul's ' offers real and lasting protection for His sheep. They can feel safe and sound

as a sheep of the
' Shepherd of the
Soul's'; the
Shepherd will look
after and protect
His sheep. They
have nothing to fear
from their enemies;
even when they are
surrounded by
them and seemingly
about to become ..

overwhelmed by their very enemies?

All of which, is why it is important to know, come to and belong to the very 'Shepherd of the Soul's?' It does not mean that there will not be hard ...

184

and difficult times , or that there will never be any problems in the life and the times of a sheep of the 'Shepherd of the Soul's?' But rather that the Shepherd will look out, help out and provide the support and care ..

His sheep need when they need it the most.

It is worthwhile noting that this Psalm; Psalm 23 is one often used at funerals? Despite this usage; I would believe that it still has much as Song of Israel, the People of the Lord God Almighty, to say to us all in our present times and days? I would go as far as saying and believing that the Psalm, is of more value to the living than those ..

187

who have passed
away and to the
other - side?

All of which
is why it is and can
be so important to
know and be found
out by the very :
' Shepherd of our
Soul's?' The very...

188

real benefits of being a sheep of the ' Shepherd of Our Soul's'; are not applicable to those who do not know and have not been found out by the : ' Shepherd of Soul's?' In some ways, we in our days have lost the imagery of Psalm 23 and the very real and constant warmth of the care and love of the : ' Shepherd of Our Soul's?' It may well be a thing that we in the 21st Century need and have a real need to rediscover for us all?

190

Our need to access this imagery of the 23rd Psalm and it's : 'Shepherd of the Soul's'; is and will be very helpful in coming to terms with the contents of the rest of this very book? Also, I would be of the belief that this helps us as we seek after and desire and pursue wholeheartedly a much more truer image and imagery of the Lord Jesus Christ as the Messiah come to the earth to save people; those who come to accept Him?

192

We all need to keep the imagery of the 23rd Psalm and that of the 'Shepherd of Soul's'; in our minds and spirits and our hearts as we seek to live in a World - at - Large which seeks to downplay the Lord Jesus Christ?

193

May yo
by the ver
ever abidi
Shepherd
Soul!

194

be found
real and
g
f your
AMEN!!!

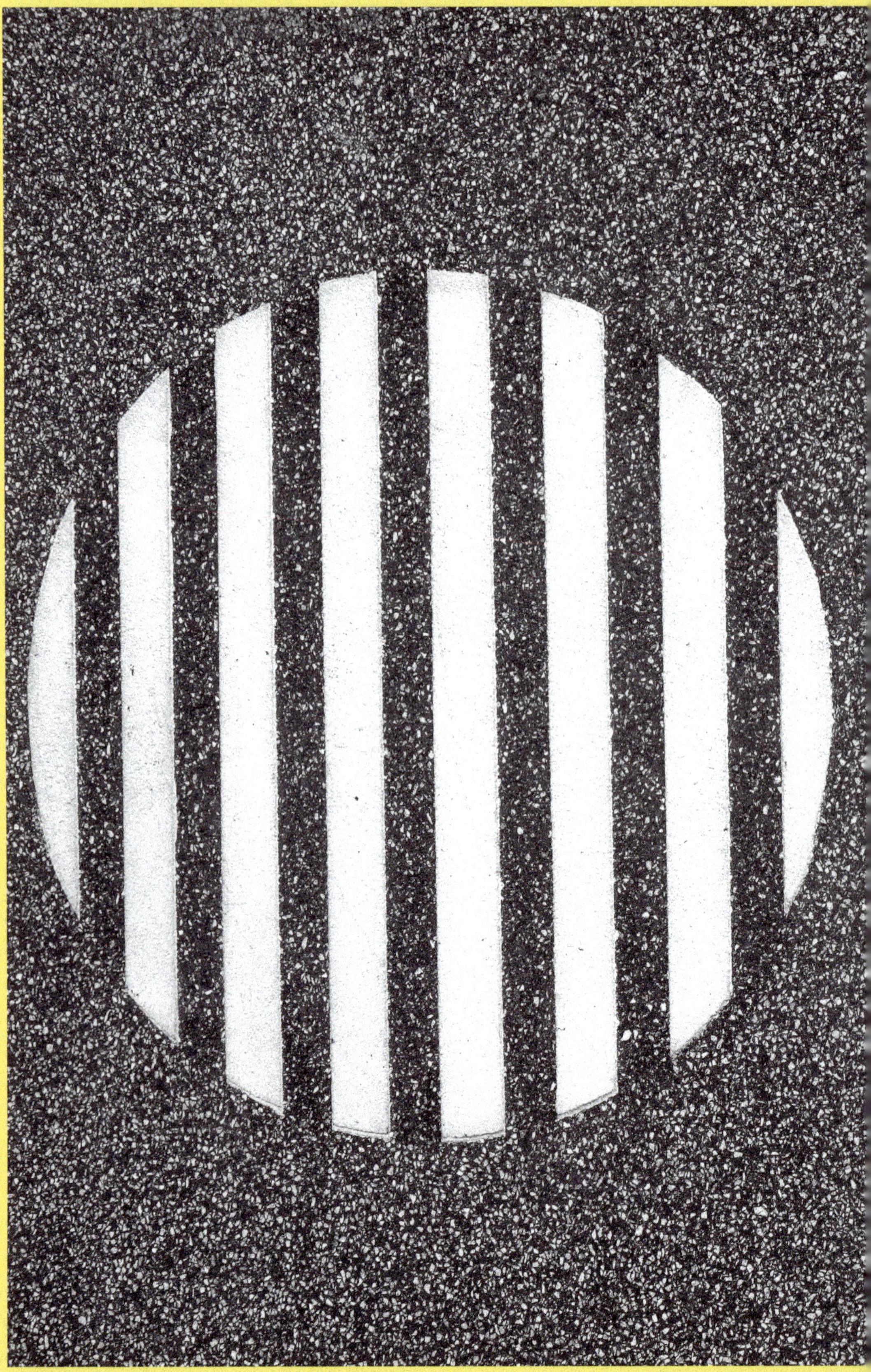

5.

John 10 : 1 - 18 and being .... 'Found By Him?'

This is a rather well known and much quoted chapter and verses on the Lord Jesus Christ as 'The Good Shepherd?' It would seem to me that in this He is aligned with the

' The Shepherd of Our Soul's' of the 23rd Psalm? Both pieces of the Word of God need and should be seen and viewed in the very light of each other ... Both have much to say to us about the One who is the 'Shepherd?'

It goes without saying that if the Lord Jesus Christ is in reality the Good Shepherd there must be one who is the Bad Shepherd .. The Evil One; Satan ?

To my reading of these very verses it is Satan who is the thief of the Sheep and the one the very sheep need to be protected from by the Lord Jesus Christ as the ' Good Shepherd?' To this end, think clearly ..

216

about the very real reality that the Bad Shepherd or Thief comes only to kill, steal and destroy! He does not come to do anything of value and worth in terms of goodness, love and care for the sheep of the flock?

217

Throughout the whole of this passage of verses from John 10 : 1 - 18 there is an implied and constant contrast made between the Thief and Bad Shepherd and The

Good Shepherd, the Lord Jesus Christ. The Good Shepherd as the Lord Jesus Christ is the One who leads to real. love and care for the sheep that are part of His flock .. Hear the promises of the

23rd Psalm ringing in your ears , mind and spirit's? The Lord Jesus Christ as The Good Shepherd is truly the 'Shepherd of Our Soul's' of the 23rd Psalm. In this all, the Lord Jesus Christ, takes much the same role and place of His Father, the Lord God Almighty .... The whole of the Godhead; the Father, the Son of God, the Lord Jesus Christ and the very Holy Spirit also have these qualities as well.... The 'Shepherd of Our Soul's'; the Father, the Son of God and the very Holy Spirit can and should be both affirmed and trusted by the sheep; their sheep of the flock.

It is worth noting;

that it is in this very passage of Scripture that the Lord Jesus Christ introduces the notion of the Good Shepherd as Himself, being prepared to die for the sheep who are His. All of which is and does by it's very nature take the whole idea of the Lord Jesus Christ as The Good Shepherd to a higher plane of meaning and insight for us all? There is and was no way that the thief would have ..

been prepared to die in the place of the sheep? Only the One who was and is the Good Shepherd; the Lord Jesus Christ was and is prepared to do this for fallen humanity. Through His death on the Cross of Calvary ..

The Good Shepherd; the One who was and is :
' The Shepherd of the Soul's ' of the 23rd Psalm was prepared to die upon the very Cross of Calvary in the place and for fallen humanity. It was He

alone who was prepared to be the 'perfect sacrifice' to the Father and in the very eyes of the Father; to pay Him for the wrongdoing; all the wrongdoing of all humanity. All of which is why we ..

227

need to be both found by Him and come to the point of acceptance of His sacrifice in our own place and stead.

In the end, it is through what the Good Shepherd did upon the very

228

Cross of Calvary; that we also get access to receiving Eternal Life with the Father, the Son of God and the very Holy Spirit; the three - in - one; Lord God Almighty? This eternal life, is life in abundance in life in the here and now and life eternal to come. The Lord Jesus Christ died upon the Cross of Calvary so that, we who are the sheep of the Good Shepherd through Faith and Belief in

Him and His works
of saving Grace
upon the Cross of
Calvary for us. may
have and live an
abundant life in the
here and now? It is
life in abundance
that we are really
talking about and
the Lord Jesus
Christ is the One ..

231

who brings the abundant life for His sheep; you and me as His sheep; in the here and now? Abundant life is on show because the Father, the Son of God and the very Holy Spirit do everything in the ..

232

form of abundance? They do not do things and life in scarcity ... and lack; remember that the Lord God Almighty, the Father, the Son of God and the very Holy Spirit , is in the end, the Creator Lord God Almighty?

This should not be seen as the so - called ' Prosperity Gospel ?' But the simple reality , is that, in the end if we as the very sheep of the flock of the Lord Jesus Christ have low; ...

very low and lowly expectations of what the Lord Jesus Christ can and will do in our lives then we should not be too surprised if that is what we receive from Him? I believe in the Lord

Jesus Christ, the Father and the very Holy Spirit who can more than we ever expect meet our needs and more? In the end, it is all about the Faith and Belief that one operates in?

236

Also; at times we simply do not ask for what we require and need at any given time and moment in time? May we be the sheep of the abundant pastures of the Lord God Almighty !

Finally, the Lord Jesus Christ was always looking for and foreshadowing that there would be sheep who were not already His sheep and He made provision for them as well. Many would see this as pointing to the very inclusion of the sheep who were Gentiles and who were not of the people of the Lord God Almighty; the Jewish people? All of which; fits in

with the overall
theme and themes of
this very book:
' Found By Him?' I
would be of the
belief that the Lord
Jesus Christ and the
Spirit of Christ, the
very Holy Spirit are
always on the
lookout for people
who are not already

240

the very sheep of the flock of the Lord Jesus Christ, the very Son of God! In the end, He pursues and makes overtures to those who are far away and very removed from His very flock of sheep?

241

The very text of John 10 : 1 - 18 ends on the high note of ; the very reality of the Lord Jesus Christ choosing to die for the sheep of the flock; His sheep and those who ....

242

would become His sheep? Freely, freely the Lord Jesus Christ gave up His own life upon the very Cross of Calvary for the wrongdoing of all humanity ... For His sheep and those who were far off !

243

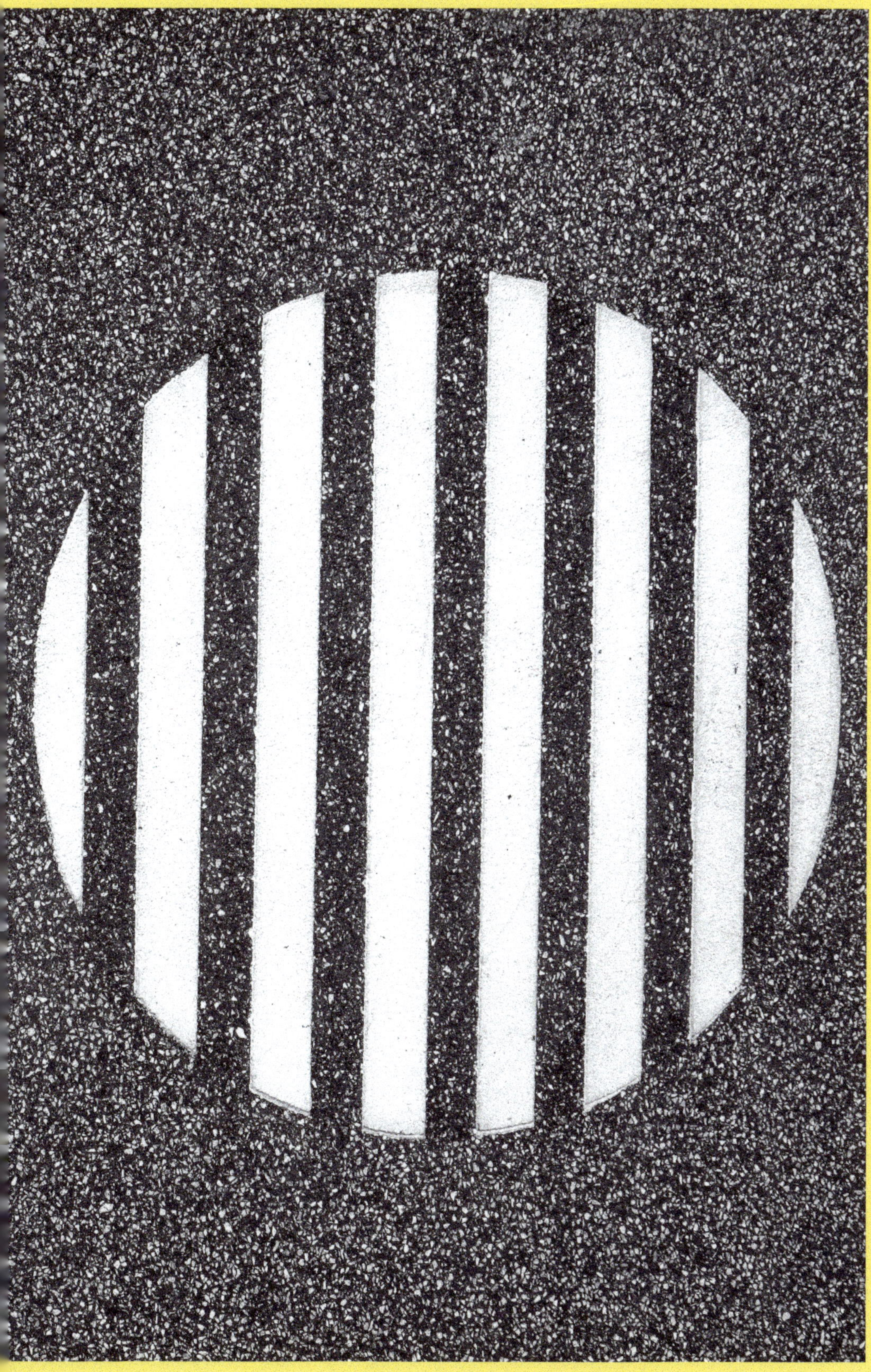

6.

Luke 15 : 1 - 7 and being :
'Found By Him?'

It is at this point in this point in this book that we will get real serious; in that, these verses are what the book is all about ; the Lost Sheep? Also, it is the reasoning as to why to spend time with people who are not already sheep; or people who once used to be sheep but have lost their way.

It is so easy to become a lost sheep in the world of the 21st Century? You may be thinking that could never happen to me but the reality , is that, the world, the flesh and the devil continue to hound the one who is as sheep! But what will the ' Shepherd of Our Soul's and ..

263

the Good Shepherd do and say when we as a sheep get lost? These verses from Luke 15 : 1 - 7 outline what the Lord Jesus Christ as the Shepherd will do when a sheep of His flock is lost. He as the ..

Good Shepherd and the ' Shepherd of the Soul's' seeks after and actively hunts for the whereabouts of the sheep that is lost. The Good Shepherd is not ever at peace while He is not ...

seeking out the sheep that is lost from His flock!

It's interesting; that the Shepherd leaves behind the other sheep who are safe and found and He goes after the sheep that is ...

266

lost? The ninety - nine in the parable that the Lord Jesus Christ are not abandoned by the Shepherd; they are still on His heart and mind but He knows that they will not wander off like the sheep that is lost! I would go as far as saying that the very Presence of the Good Shepherd ; the' Shepherd of our Soul's' abides and remains with the rest of the flock of His sheep. This is very important to grasp and come to some understanding of? The Lord Jesus Christ and His very Presence abides and remains with the whole of His flock of sheep and not just those that are in reality the lost sheep! The One who is the Good Shepherd can and should be trusted !

At this point I want to take a rather divergent tack and think about the flock of sheep and why the 'outcasts and those who have done the wrong thing' are part of the flock? It would seem to me, that the reasoning that the Lord Jesus Christ had behind this , is that, of the very reality of all the sheep .... and non - sheep being created in the 'imago deo'; the very Image of God? This would be

271

the reasoning behind why the Lord Jesus Christ could view those who were ' outcasts ' and those who had done the wrong thing in the very eyes of the Lord God Almighty as

272

being nothing
more than lost
sheep
themselves?

Therefore,
one could say that
everybody is a
sheep and is
created in the
image of the very

273

image of the :
' Shepherd of Our Soul's ' but some lose their way and get lost from the very flock of the 'Good Shepherd?' I am not talking about 'Universalism?' but rather I am focused on the very reality

274

of the very sheep and people of the whole of the world and the creation being created in the very ' Imago Deo'; the Image of God? Therefore, it is like they are just back Home to the Father, the Son of God and the very Holy Spirit?

Therefore, this is why the Lord Jesus Christ as both the ' Good Shepherd and the Shepherd of Our Soul's' ; did value and give worth and dignity to all people?All of which is why the

'Good Shepherd' would seek after one, even just one lost sheep of His flock and even outside of His very flock of sheep!

The Lord Jesus Christ as the ' Good Shepherd' was and is always concerned for ...

those who are on the very margins of the World - at - Large and viewed as being the ones who are the outcasts of the World and not given their rightful value, dignity and worth as being created in the very image of the ...

278

Shepherd ... Sheep created in the very Image of the 'Good Shepherd' ; you heard it right ... the 'Imago Deo'; is in play at all times ... it may well be corrupted and distorted but it still is there ?

279

In conclusion to this chapter, it is worth noting and highlighting that the ' Good Shepherd' rightly wants the finding and the very return of a sheep that has been lost to be celebrated much; He wants us as His sheep of His flock to have a whole lot of rejoicing at the very finding and the return of a wayward sheep to His flock? I would also widen this to include those who are not usually included or thought of as being the very sheep of the flock of the 'Good Shepherd ?' Much akin to the return and the very Homecoming of the Prodigal Son to His Father! He too, had lost his way but eventually came back to his mind and made a very real Homecoming to his Father and family; the flock of sheep as in this parable.

The Lord Jesus

283

Christ as the very 'Shepherd of Our Soul's' ; the 'Good Shepherd of John 10 '; will always have a very real concern and default position that seeks out and cares for the lost and those on the ..

very margins of the World - at - Large and it's various Nation states and Societies? He will always as the One who is truly the 'Good Shepherd' seek out after those who are wayward and lost?

What a joyous occasion it is to be ' Found By Him?' It is like the ultimate Homecoming that one could and can possibly ever have ... A return to the very flock of the ..

286

' Good Shepherd';
the very
' Shepherd of Our
Soul's of the 23rd
Psalm?' We all
have a need, a
very real need to
be ' Found By
Him?' May you
truly be 'Found By
Him?' Amen!!!

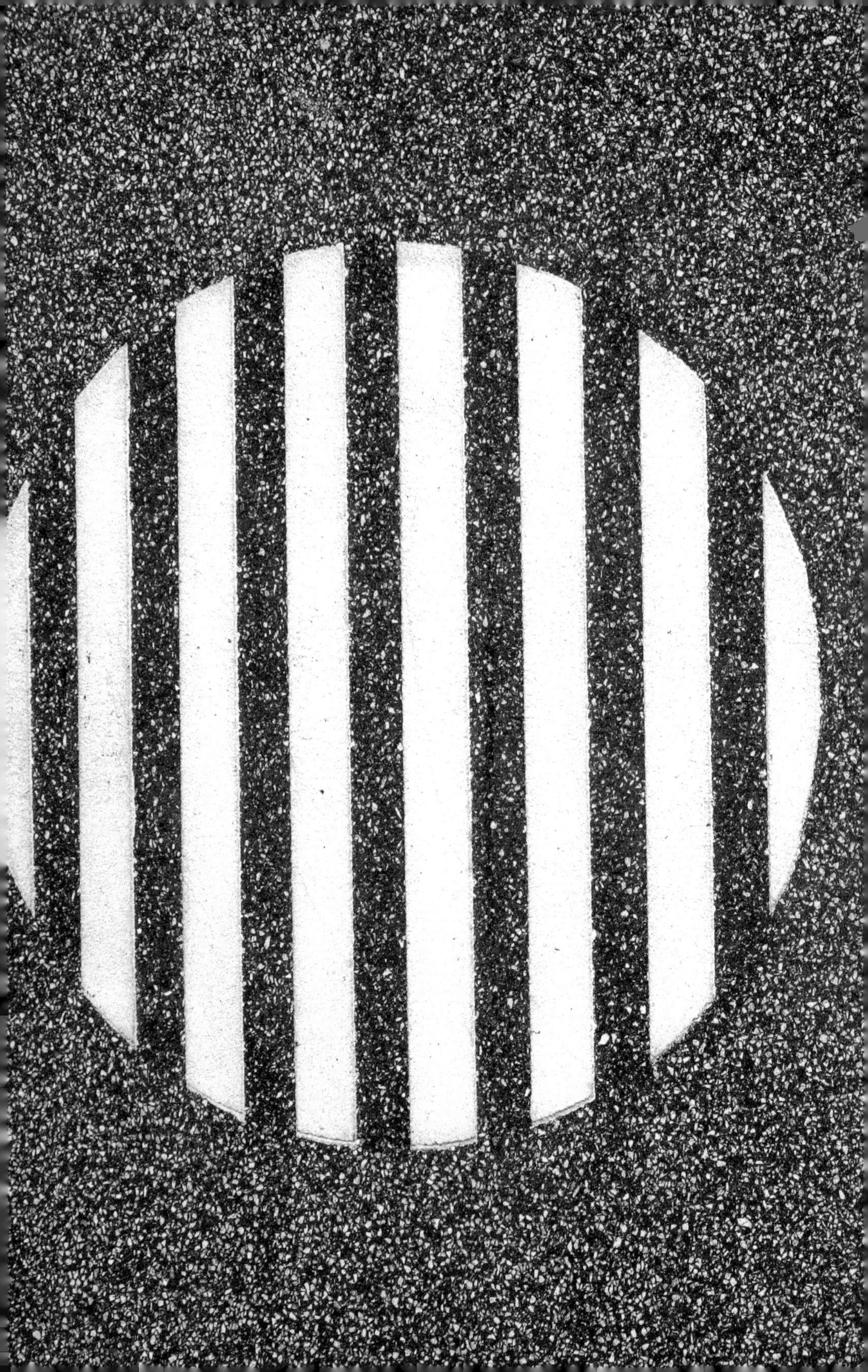

May ...

Be 'Found

You ...

By Him?'

301

7.

EPILOGUE

This book
has sought to
consider
being 'Found
By Him?' To
do this it has
looked at ...

Psalm 23, John 10 : 1 - 18 and Luke 15 : 1 - 7? They are all concerned with the One

who is both the ....
' Shepherd of Our Soul's;' and the 'Good .... Shepherd?' They are all

concerned with the Shepherd and His sheep and what it looks like for the One to be truly the ....

Shepherd? Also, one of them in particular thinks about what the 'Good Shepherd' ...

does when
one of the
sheep of the
flock ... His
very flock is
lost and
wayward? He
drops all He..

312

has and
seeks and
hunts after
the lost and
wayward
sheep ... In
the same
way the Lord

Jesus Christ as the One who is truly the ' Good Shepherd' goes after the lost and wayward ? He

is and
always will
be concerned
and have a
real desire
and affection
for those
sheep who ...

315

are the very
sheep who
are the lost
and the
wayward ,
the sheep
who are
dispossessed

316

and on the very margins of the World - at - large and it's Nation states ...The desires of the 'Good Shepherd' .....

317

have not and
will never
change ... the
' Good
Shepherd '
will never
stop seeking
after those ..

318

who are lost,
wayward,
dispossessed
and on the
very margins
and fringes
of the World -
at - Large ?

If we
are sheep
that are lost
and wayward;
may we too
come Home to
the ' Good ...

320

Shepherd' the
One who is
and always
will be the
very
'Shepherd of
Our Soul's?'
We all have a

need to be :

'Found
By
HIM.'

322

The

Author :

John C Burt.

JOHN HAS BEEN A FOLLOWER OF THE LORD JESUS CHRIST FOR FORTY - FOUR YEARS!

JOHN LOVES THE ODD CUP OF COFFEE .. STRONG AND HOT AND EVEN DARE I SAY BITTER....

327

MY PRAYER, IS THAT, IF YOU ARE A LOST AND A WAYWARD SHEEP YOU ..

328

MAY BE
'FOUND BY
HIM'; THE
GOOD
SHEPHERD
AND THE
SHEPHERD OF

329

OUR SOULS'?
TAKE TIME
NOW TO TURN
YOUR OWN
HEART AND
YOUR OWN
SPIRIT TO
THE 'GOOD ...
330

SHEPHERD'; THE ONE WHO IS TRULY THE 'SHEPHERD OF OUR SOUL'S?'

AMEN AND AMEN!

331

A PRAYER
YOU COULD
PRAY IS :DEAR
LORD JESUS
CHRIST.
THANK YOU
FOR BEING MY
SHEPHERD ...

332

THE ONE WHO
IS TRULY THE
SHEPHERD OF
MY SOUL!
WHEN I GET
LOST MAY I BE
FOUND BY
YOU! WE ALL

333

ARE SHEEP WHO ARE PRONE TO WANDER AND GET LOST IN THE CARES AND CONCERNS OF

334

OUR VERY
EVERYDAY
LIVES UNDER
THE GAZE OF
THE LORD!
MAY YOU
FIND ME !!!
AMEN !!!

335

MAY YOU BE:
' FOUND BY
HIM ?'

348

Lightning Source UK Ltd.
Milton Keynes UK
UKHW051216220321
380763UK00007B/92